Elemental

a Journey through Lent with the Earth

Paul Galbreath (signature)

Daily Devotional Readings for the Lenten Season

art by
Tara Taber

text by
Paul Galbreath

Parson's Porch Books

Elemental: A Journey through Lent with the Earth

ISBN: Softcover 978-1-0880-5014-9

Copyright © 2022 by Tara Taber and Paul Galbreath

This work was made possible through a Vital Worship Grant from the Calvin Institute of Christian Worship, Grand Rapids, Michigan, with funds provided by Lilly Endowment Inc.

Parson's Porch Books is an imprint of Parson's Porch & Company (PP&C) in Cleveland, Tennessee. PP&C is an innovative organization which raises money by publishing books of noted authors, representing all genres. Its face and voice is David Tullock (dtullock@parsonsporch.com).

Parson's Porch & Company turns books into bread & milk by sharing its profits with the poor.

www.parsonsporch.com.

Elemental

A Journey through Lent with the Earth

4

Introduction

While it is not unusual to reflect on Lent as a pilgrimage from Ash Wednesday to Easter Sunday, this devotional book diverges from traditional types of this journey by inviting us to turn our attention to the earth as a place where we encounter signs of the divine presence. The reflection for each day draws on a Scriptural reference that relates to an element from nature: Sunday – Plants/Grain; Monday – Sky; Tuesday – Wind; Wednesday – Soil; Thursday – Water; Friday – Trees; Saturday – Rocks.

These reflections were inspired by two important experiences: 1) I participated in a prayer walk led by indigenous women that followed the path of the Cayuhoga River (for more on this incredible movement see nibiwalk.org). I remain grateful to Sharon Day for her generous and inspiring leadership as she works to invite us to honor and respect water; and 2) a walk I led from the ocean to the sanctuary of First Presbyterian Church in Newport, Oregon that allowed us to explore the connection between our commitment to earth care and our baptismal vows. I am particularly indebted to Rev. Kelsey Ingalls for her enthusiastic participation and support. The Newport walk provided the basis for the artwork by Tara Taber that accompanies these reflections.

_____

_____

_____

_____

_____

_____

Ash Wednesday

"Remember you are earth and earth you shall become."

These words taken from the creation story in Genesis 3 accompany the action of being marked by the sign of the cross on Ash Wednesday. It is a way to remind us of our limits – these days of our lives that we share on this fragile planet. This day invites us to look at ourselves as part of the earth, taken from the ground, breathed into life by the gift of air, and returned to the earth. The season of Lent invites us on a journey to reconnect with the earth. It is a chance to no longer look at ourselves apart from the earth, but to see ourselves as deeply part of the earth, the source of our life, and the place to which we will return. It is a challenging word and also a word of hope since our future is bound up with the future of the earth. Caring for the earth is a way of caring for ourselves.

We are invited this Lenten season to reflect on our relationship with the earth and to choose ways to act that care for the earth. It is a journey that we share together as we travel towards the hope of sharing resurrection life for ourselves and for all of creation. You are asked to commit to new practices of earth care during the coming weeks – a way of building new habits that show that baptismal life includes a commitment to care for the earth as central to Christian discipleship. For example, you may choose to focus on conserving your use of water or decide to pick up trash in a park near you each week.

Consider that your earth care practice is also a form of embodied prayer – a way to work for the healing of the earth.

_____

_____

_____

_____

_____

_____

Day 2

"In the day that God made the earth and the heavens, when no plant of the field was yet in the earth and no herb of the field had yet sprung up— for God had not caused it to rain upon the earth, and there was no one to till the ground; but a stream would rise from the earth, and water the whole face of the ground." Genesis 2:4b-6

Our journey begins by following the way of the water. In the stories of creation in Genesis, water comes as the gift of God. It rises up out of the earth to provide the source of fertility and productivity that allows life to come forth. Water is a precious resource from which all of life comes. Each day, we depend on it for our basic needs: drinking, bathing, growing food and plants, cleaning, recreation. We use water in our worship services to celebrate the grace that God offers us as beloved children of God. The water of baptism welcomes us to share life in a community where we promise to care for our neighbors and for God's creation.

An important step on this baptismal journey is to grow in our knowledge of the water that we depend on for daily life. What is your local watershed? What is the closest river or body of water? A renewed emphasis on discipleship and earth care invites us to find ways to recognize our dependence on the water that is near us, and which provides us life. When we recognize our relationship to the water, then we look for ways to honor and care for this basic element. A starting place is to take a photo of water near us and include it in our prayers each day. We can put our prayers into action by volunteering at local organizations that are working to clean up local rivers and habitats.

_____

_____

_____

_____

_____

_____

Day 3

"And God planted a garden in Eden, in the east; and there God put the man whom he had formed. Out of the ground God made to grow every tree that pleasant to the sight and food for food, the tree of life also in the midst of the garden, and the tree of the knowledge of good and evil." Genesis 2:8-9

From oxygen to food, trees provide the basic resources on which our lives depend. The creation story in Genesis makes it clear that we have always recognized trees as God's gift that brings beauty and sustenance to the world. It is no accident that the description of Eden places a tree in the middle of the garden as a source of life and a resource for knowledge. Trees show us the history of life on this planet. They provide records of natural disasters, and they adapt to changes in the ecological environment. Recent research points to the ways that trees communicate with one another. Their root systems run deep and wide into the ground and they send out signals of upcoming danger.

Trees also provide shelter for vast arrays of habitat from the birds and wildlife that nest in their branches to the diverse forms of flora that grow on their tree trunks and in and around their roots. As humans, we are keenly aware of the shade they provide on hot summer days and the relief that they give us from howling winds. What are you doing to care for trees in your neighborhood? How are you involved in preserving habitat that will allow trees to flourish and provide us with the oxygen that we need to survive? Our reflections on the earth during this season of Lent invite us to this vision from Genesis where we find our place in caring for the trees that give us life.

_____

_____

_____

_____

_____

_____

Day 4

"So Jacob rose early in the morning, and he took the stone that he had put under his head and set it up for a pillar and poured oil on the top of it. He called that place Bethel." Genesis 28:18-19

Jacob dreamed of a ladder that reached up to heaven.

The angels who used this ladder brought a message of promise and hope to him: God will go with you and guide you on your travels and on your return to this place. This dream was so striking that when Jacob woke up that he was determined to mark this time and place. He took the rock that he slept on and anointed it with oil and named the place Bethel, the house of God.

There's an interesting lesson for us in this story. Like Jacob, we encounter God in unlikely and unexpected places. Sometimes it is in our dreams, sometimes in our encounters with friends or strangers, sometimes in our walks through the woods. In these times, we discover God's promise to accompany us on our journey. Maybe we would be wise to mark these moments in our lives. Jacob takes a stone and pours oil over it as a sign of his awareness that he had experienced God's presence surrounded by this stuff (rocks and dirt and trees) in this particular place. Every time he passed by this place in the coming years, he stopped and looked at the rock and remembered God's promise. When we keep rocks on our fireplace mantles or in our windowsills as memories of our experiences of God's presence, they are there to remind us that we are not alone on this journey. This is one way in which the rocks call out to us and remind us that God accompanies us each step of the way.

_____

_____

_____

_____

_____

_____

_____

1st Sunday in Lent

"You visit the earth and water it, you greatly enrich it; the river of God is full of water; you provide the people with grain, for so you have prepared it." Psalm 65:9

All of life is a gift from God. On this journey through Lent, we are pausing each day to look around us at the earth in order that we might more clearly recognize the ways in which our life is integrally connected with and dependent on the gifts of this good earth that God creates and loves. The Psalmist invites us to praise God for two remarkable, lifegiving reasons: 1) by remembering God's faithful presence in our pasts we see the source of hope that continues to sustain our lives; and 2) by looking at the world around us we see the amazing ways in which God provides for our basic needs. The first reason offered by the Psalmist roots our lives within a community that shares these stories of God's presence as ways to sustain our hope in difficult times. Do you remember when by the grace of God we survived these experiences? Here the past frames our expectations and prepares us to anticipate God's presence especially in the midst of challenges. "By awesome deeds you answer us with deliverance, O God of our salvation" (vs. 5). The second reason invites us to observe the world around us and discern God's presence in the earth and water which allow the grain to grow so that we will have enough to eat.

On our walks during this season of Lent, we are learning to look at the signs of life in the world around us that are there to sustain and encourage us: the beauty of the flowers as they bloom, the wild berries that that grow along the roadside, and the fields of grain that provide food for us to eat are all signs of the divine presence woven into creation.

_____

_____

_____

_____

_____

_____

Day 6

"God said, 'This is the sign of the covenant that I make between me and you and every living creature that is with you, for all future generations: I have set my bow in the clouds, and it shall be a sign of the covenant between me and the earth.'" Genesis 9:12-13

When I listened to the story of Noah and the ark as a child, my favorite part was the descriptions of the animals going two by two into the giant boat. I loved to imagine them galloping, creeping, and flying on board to create a community on board this vast ship. At the time, I never really worried about the fate of the small animals in light of the ravenous appetites of the larger carnivores. Instead, we played with the cutout shapes of the animals as we placed them on the cruise ship together.

The story of Noah and the ark though is not simply a tale of unlikely survival. For ancient Israel it provides an assurance of God's faithful presence in the midst of difficult challenges in our lives. At the center of this narrative is a declaration that the sky provides a sign of God's covenant with us. The light of the sun refracted through the raindrops creates a rainbow. To this day when I see a rainbow in the sky, it takes my breath away. The beauty of the colors splashed in an arc across the sky prompts me to stop and reflect on the ways that I am responding to and caring for the signs of God's presence in the world around me. During this season of Lent, we are pausing each day to pay attention to the ways that the earth invites us to awaken to God's promises on display in the sky above us.

_____

_____

_____

_____

_____

_____

Day 7

"In the beginning when God created the heavens and the earth, the earth was a formless void and darkness covered the face of the deep, while a wind from God swept over the face of the waters."
Genesis 1:1-2

The first sign of God's presence on the earth was the wind blowing across the water. These opening words from the creation story in Genesis provide us with a picture of God's activity that brings life forth on this planet. In this primordial time of darkness, it is the wind whisking over the water that is the first movement of creation. Life starts with the wind of God's breath blowing across the earth. In Genesis 2, human life emerges in a similar way. God forms man out of the earth and breathes into him the breath of life (vs. 7). From this account, all of life including our own comes from the divine wind that breathes all creation into life.

Maybe this is why we pause when we watch the wind blowing the trees or rippling across a pond. The wind points us towards the presence of the Creator who continues to bring life forth around us. On our journey through Lent, the changing nature of the wind will catch us by surprise. On those days when the wind is at our back, let us pray that the Spirit will push us to work for justice for all of creation. On the days, when we face strong headwinds may the Spirit give us strength to persevere. On every day, let us give thanks for the gift of wind as the first sign of God's presence that creates, sustains, and weaves all of life together. This text from Genesis is a reminder of our dependence on God and our interdependence with all of creation.

_____

_____

_____

_____

_____

_____

Day 8

"The earth is the Lord's and all that is in it, the world, and those who live in it." Psalm 24:1

Have you ever wondered what it means to own a piece of land? When we buy property it comes with certain rights and responsibilities. We are allowed to develop the property in accordance with local zoning regulations, but there are also basic requirements to care for the land and to respond when issues arise (a tree falls across a sidewalk and the owner is responsible for clearing the path).

The Psalmist offers a different perspective on this issue of land ownership. All of the earth belongs to God and every-thing and everyone on this planet. It is such a grandiose claim that we often simply skip over it. It's fine to read in church occasionally, but clearly the Psalmist was not concerned about making the monthly mortgage payment to stay in their house on the hillside. What would happen to our perspective though if we allowed the Psalmist to serve as a corrective to the ways that we think about "our land"? When we begin to think more expansively about the earth as more than a commodity to buy and sell, then we start to see ourselves in a different light. I can no longer claim to be in charge of this estate (note the irony of the expression "lord of the manor"), but instead see myself as belonging to God and as part of all God's creation. This sense of solidarity with the earth prompts me to act in different ways. Rather than seeing the land as mine to do with as I choose, I begin to see my place in living in harmony with this land which provides a place for me to live. Partnering with the earth is an important step on our Lenten journey as we find our role on God's good earth.

Day 9

"From your lofty abode, you water the mountains.
The earth is satisfied with the fruit of your work."
Psalm 104:13

The clouds open up and the rain pours down. The water soaks the trees, gathers in puddles, and runs down the hillsides as it slowly seeps into the ground. In this frequent act, the earth is renewed. Rain provides us with the water that we drink and the water that is needed to grow our food. Our gardens and farms rely on the rain that nourishes the ground and allows the plants to grow.

The Psalmist looks at the world and recognizes it as an opportunity to give thanks. The goodness of the earth prompts a response: "Bless the Lord, O my soul,. . . you are very great" (vs. 1). A praise song breaks out in thanksgiving to God the creator and provider of the earth. It is helpful to note the ways that our lives are interdependent with the well-being of the earth. As the earth flourishes, we recognize our place in creation and the ways in which we rely on and benefit from the well-being of the earth.

John Calvin wrote in the preface to a French translation of the Bible: "It is evident that all creatures, from those in the heavens to those under the earth are able to act as witnesses and messengers of God's glory. .... For the little birds that sing, sing of God; the beasts clamor for God; the elements dread God; the mountains echo God, and the fountains and flowing waters wink at God."

This Lenten journey offers us the chance to more clearly. acknowledge the ways in which our actions damage the environment. Taking inventory of and responsibility for our choices provides us with a chance to repent and change our ways so that we can participate in the healing of creation. As we turn to the earth, we can join with the birds and beasts and the fountains and flowing waters in giving thanks to the creator and sustainer of life.

23

_____

_____

_____

_____

_____

_____

Day 10

"They [Happy are those who] are like trees planted by streams of water, which yield their fruit in its season and their leaves do not wither. In all that they do, they prosper." Psalm 1:3

Have you ever wanted to be a tree - tall and strong with deep roots that run far and wide into the earth? Have you longed to provide sustenance for those around you and to remain vibrant year around? This is the vision that the Psalmist provides us of life that is rooted in God. Happiness, a flourishing life, resembles a mighty evergreen that provides a home for birds and wildlife. Happiness is like a healthy apple tree where the blossoms grow into apples that are harvested and shared with our neighbors.

We can learn to prosper, says the Psalmist, by paying attention to the trees around us. Trees offer us not only the physical benefits of shade, oxygen, produce, and shelter, they also model lessons in flourishing and happiness. Trees rely on the availability of water, earth, and sun in order to grow. As they grow, they adjust to the conditions around them. They bend towards the light and absorb the impact of windstorms.

On this Lenten journey with our eyes wide open to the world around us, this psalm invites us to claim the truths of both scripture and nature in the ways that they point us towards life. For the Psalmist, our grounding in God's Word will cause us to prosper like the trees that we walk under each day. As our roots take hold and extend into the earth and as we draw on the water that provides us with the gift of life, we will begin to resemble the trees that show us how to prosper and thrive.

_____

_____

_____

_____

_____

_____

Day 11

"When your children ask their parents in time to come, 'What do these stones mean?' then you shall let your children know, 'Israel crossed over the Jordan here on dry ground.'" Joshua 4:21-22

Joshua helped the Israelites set up twelve large stones at Gilgal as a monument that created a place to remember the time when they passed through the Jordan River into the promised land. For the Israelites, this story remains central to their identity as God's covenant people. The crossing of the Jordan River offers a direct parallel to the Exodus account of crossing the Red Sea and the liberation from slavery in Egypt. The twelve stones that are erected on the site near the Jordan River memorialize the twelve tribes of Israel who were led by Moses through the long journey in the wilderness and who are now led by Joshua across the river into the promised land. This ancient stone sculpture was created for two important reasons: 1) so that the people would stop long enough and gather up the rocks as a way of recognizing how far they had come together by the grace of God; and 2) to create a place where they could return with their children and grandchildren and tell the story of their journey into this new territory.

This story from Joshua reminds us of the way in which rocks can help us mark significant moments in our lives. Their physical presence can help us remember a time and place when we encountered God's presence. Like the ancient Israelites, taking time to create a rock garden may be a form of embodied prayer where we pause and give thanks for God's presence in bringing us through difficult times. Similarly, keeping these rocks in our gardens and yards prompts us to recall and share these stories and to live each day with gratitude for God's protection.

_____

_____

_____

_____

_____

_____

2nd Sunday in Lent

"She did not know that it was I who gave her the grain, the wine, and the oil." Hosea 2:8

Taken for granted: this is the tale in which Hosea pronounces to the Israelites that they have taken God for granted. They have turned their attention elsewhere and become preoccupied with other concerns. Their lives are busy with activities, and they have forgotten God is the source of life. When they gather to eat their meals, they no longer recall that God provides the grain that produces bread that they share, the olive oil with which they cook and eat, and the wine in the chalices that they drink. These basic ingredients of the ancient Mediterranean diet were harvested from the land. Hosea's words are a cry of sorrow from God that humans have turned away from the Creator.

While we may offer a brief prayer before our meals, I wonder how deep our gratitude grows for the food and drink on our tables. How often do we take for granted that our refrigerators are full or that we have choices about what and how much we eat each day? It is easy for me to pay little attention to the bread that I eat for breakfast each morning, to rush through the meal and hurry on to the tasks of the day. During this season of Lent, we are turning to look at the earth more closely so that we will see how closely we are connected to the world around us and in doing so will also more readily recognize God's presence in the gifts of creation. By pausing and opening our eyes to the sun that comes streaming through our windows and our ears to the rain that patters on our roofs, we start the slow process of awakening to the wonder of creation through which God provides us with our basic needs.

_____

_____

_____

_____

_____

_____

_____

Day 13

"God brought Abram outside and said, 'Look toward heaven and count the stars, if you are able to count them.' Then God said to him, 'So shall your descendants be.'" Genesis 15:5

On a clear evening, it is always inspiring to go outside and look up at the stars. Against the vastness of the universe, we gain a different sense of ourselves as we stand beneath the shimmering stars. We feel small and insignificant as we look up at the constellations that have served as navigational guides to travelers across the centuries.

The story of Abram's call provides us with a contrasting map of emotional responses. For Abram, looking to the night sky provides him with a source of hope and connection. Our text from Genesis portrays this experience coming at a time of transition in Abram's life as he wonders what will become of his life. Without children, he and his wife wonder who will remember them. Precisely at this point in Abram's vision, God urges him to walk outside and look up to the night sky. The countless number of stars twinkling in the sky represent the legacy of Abram's life whose descendants will be too many to count.

For Abram, the stars represent God's promise of a future that is brighter than he can imagine. Following this vision, each night when Abram looks up at the bright stars that shimmer above the desert sky, he remembers God's promise to provide for his future.

This story from Genesis offers us the chance to see ourselves in a new light. When we stare up at the stars, we can see not just our small place in a vast universe but also the promise God makes that our futures are bound up in the stars. This sense of deep relationality is woven through the fabric of the universe. Our care for the earth is a way of extending care to ourselves and to the future that God reveals to us.

_____

_____

_____

_____

_____

_____

Day 14

"Then Moses stretched out his hand over the sea. The Lord drove the sea back by a strong east wind all night and turned the sea into dry land; and the waters were divided." Exodus 14:21

The exodus narrative is one of the foundational stories of identity for the Israelites. This text describes their release from the bondage of slavery in ancient Egypt and their escape from the armies of Pharaoh as they cross the Red Sea.

Throughout this journey, Moses serves as the leader who fights for their freedom and who urges the Hebrew people to trust God to lead them into a new future. No matter what obstacles the people face, Moses implores God to find a way to deliver them from danger and oppression. As they gather on the banks of the Red Sea, the people cry out in fear that there is no way for them to move forward. In this dangerous moment, it is the wind that blows through the sea and creates a path for the people to escape. As we saw the wind as God's first act of creation in Genesis, the wind here provides God's act of salvation, a time of new creation as the Hebrew people experience God's liberating work in their lives.

Where do you long for freedom and a new beginning? Where do you see the liberating wind of God moving in your life? This Lenten season offers us a time of new birth – a time to connect with the gift of nature and to grow in our awareness of the divine presence that is woven throughout creation. May this divine wind create new pathways for us and lead us into God's future. As we move forward, may we join with creation in singing songs of praise to God.

_____

_____

_____

_____

_____

_____

Day 15

"The Lord loves righteousness and justice; the earth is full of the steadfast love of the Lord."
Psalm 33:5

There are special places that we love where we sense God's presence. For some, it is when they stand on a particular beach and watch the waves come rolling in from the sea. For others, it is the sight of a particular mountain or a grove of mighty trees. These places call out to us in ways that awaken us to the divine presence in the world.

The Psalmist offers a much broader perspective on God's presence: the earth is full of God's steadfast love. This fullness is not bound to a particular place but is a vision of the earth imbued with the presence of God.

This is a fully incarnational theology in which all of the earth displays God's steadfast love. It is particularly striking that this statement is not qualified by our understandings of what is beautiful, but that it claims that all land is sacred because it all reveals the love of God. Even the earth's scars provide a testimony to the steadfast love of God.

The awareness of God's presence around us is linked with a call to righteousness and justice. This Lenten journey seeks to raise our awareness of the sacredness of the earth as the place where we encounter God and in doing so we recognize our role in working for righteousness and justice. For the Psalmist, righteousness and justice are about the ways we live and act each day. How will we respond when we see the earth as a display of God's love? What will we do to protect and preserve the goodness of the earth? Today and every day offers us the opportunity to respond to God's presence around us by working for justice.

_____

_____

_____

_____

_____

_____

Day 16

"You visit the earth and water it, you greatly enrich it; the river of God is full of water; you provide the people with grain, for so you have prepared it." Psalm 65:9.

We are traveling through this season of Lent with all those who are joining this baptismal journey of following the path of the water and responding to the cries of the earth. As our awareness of the earth grows, we recognize our interdependence that is woven into the fabric of creation, and we look to act in ways that will honor and care for water which provides us with the gift of life.

As a spiritual practice, caring for the earth is a central part of our commitment to live as disciples of Jesus Christ. Today's text from Psalm 65 points to the possibility of encountering God in our actions of caring for the water sources that surround us. Note the claim embedded in this text: "You [God] visit the earth and water it." Hence as we work for cleaner water and respond to the needs of the earth, the possibility exists for us to encounter the One who visits the earth and provides us with the gift of water that sustains life on earth. To place our hands into the rivers and streams that surround us is to open ourselves up to the divine presence that brings forth life into the universe. In this psalm, the river is identified as the river of God because of the way in which it provides the nourishment that allows the grain to grow and be harvested for food. What would happen if we identified the rivers in our neighborhoods as God's rivers? How would we treat the water if we anticipated it as a place that God visits? The gift of this day invites us to experience the world around as a place to meet the One who is the source of life.

_____

_____

_____

_____

_____

_____

Day 17

"O sing to God a new song; sing to God, all the earth. . . . Then shall all the trees of the forest sing for joy." Psalm 96:1;and 12b

Today on our journey through Lent, we are singing traveling songs. When our songs name God's faithfulness that sustains us, then they resonate deeply within us. Take a moment to remember the times and places where God's grace has kept you going. Recall the times of crisis and brokenness where you had nowhere to turn. In these moments, we finally realize our dependence on God. In these times our prayers reflect our deep longing for God's grace to wash over us and for us to see ourselves as God's beloved children. It's important for us to keep these times and places at the center of our songs of praise.

Today is the day for us to learn a new song. This invitation comes from the Psalmist who invites us to sing a new song and to bless God. It is a song that grows out of our experiences of God's goodness and all of the ways in which our lives depend upon God's grace each and every day. For the Psalmist, though, this song of thanksgiving is not a solo, but is a shared chorus. This new song has a harmony that is shared by all of the earth. This song brings joy to both the heavens and the earth. The sea joins by adding its roar and the fields find their own part in the chorus. When this song comes to fruition in our lives, then the trees of the forest will sing for joy. As we see and live into our connection to the earth, then this new song with the harmony of the trees begins to take root in our lives.

_____

_____

_____

_____

_____

_____

Day 18

"God alone is my rock and my salvation, my fortress; I shall never be shaken." Psalm 62:2

The Bible explores all kinds of images for God: breath, spirit, father, mother hen. The Psalmist tries out a metaphor that is often overlooked. God is like a rock. We do not often consider positive attributes of rocks. We talk about stumbling blocks, rocky soil that won't produce crops, and how rocks weigh us down so that we can't move forward. It's interesting then to note other ways to reflect on rocks. In a time of turmoil, the Psalmist feels under duress, and offers this song of quiet hope. The refrain comes twice over the course of twelve verses: "God alone is my rock and my salvation." No matter what may come his way, the Psalmist expresses a confident trust that even in times when he cannot clearly hear or see God's presence that God will surely bring deliverance.

God is "my mighty rock, my refuge is in God" (vs. 7).

It is interesting to note how some aspects of creation readily evoke a sense of awe that we are in the presence of the divine. We stop and gape as the water cascades down a mighty waterfall or we stare up at an ancient redwood tree. Rocks, though, rarely catch us by surprise in this kind of way. Maybe rocks have an important lesson for us to learn during this Lenten season about all that is ordinary around us that we so often take for granted. Pick up a rock and hold it in your hand. Rocks are solid and sturdy. Rock walls and fences last for centuries. The image of God as rock points to permanence and reliability. Let us give thanks today for the gift of rocks and the way in which they point us to new dimensions of God's presence in our world.

_____

_____

_____

_____

_____

_____

42

3rd Sunday in Lent

"You cause the grass to grow for the cattle, and plants for people to use, to bring forth food from the earth, and wine to gladden the human heart, oil to make the face shine, and bread to strengthen the human heart." Psalm 104:14-15

Life is to enjoy! The Psalmist invites us to experience a joyful life in the presence of God who creates and provides for us. What is striking about the language of this Psalm is the way that it pushes past merely surviving to point to the possibility of flourishing. This full life is vividly portrayed in descriptive terms about what God gives us to sustain our lives and invites us to share with one another. We drink the wine that comes from the grapes that grow in the sun because it makes us happy. We use the oil from the olives to make our faces shine. We break the bread together and eat it to strengthen our hearts. These gifts of God bring joy to our lives.

Sometimes we become accustomed to simply trudging through each day. As our gratitude for God's grace deepens, then we begin to see the many ways in which we are blessed by all that sustains us. Today, though, the Psalmist nudges us a bit further on our journey of gratitude so that we will see and relish the beauty and goodness that God provides for us.

Jesus declares to us that he came so that we may have life and have it more abundantly. Hence this journey through Lent begins with awareness of God's goodness that surrounds us and sustains us, grows within us as thanksgiving taking shape in our lives, and becomes a joyful song that accompanies us through our days. Take time today to find opportunities to experience this vision of abundant living.

_____

_____

_____

_____

_____

_____

Day 20

"When I look at your heavens, the work of your fingers, the moon and the stars that you have established; what are human beings that you are mindful of them, mortals that you care for them?"
Psalm 8:3-4

The Psalmist describes the world as belonging to God.

The heavens are yours, God, the work of your hands. The moon and stars are the result of your creation. Here the earth is pictured in relational terms as deeply bound to the divine life. The beauty of the world points to God's presence that is evident throughout creation. The sky, moon, and stars are not described as independent entities, but as that which discloses the Creator's desire and commitment to life.

For Presbyterians, the Brief Statement of Faith begins with these words: "In life and death, we belong to God." This summary of Christian faith starts with an acknowledgment of our dependence on God for the source of all life. It is an acknowledgment that we are not masters of our own fate, but that in Christ we turn to recognize our reliance on God. The Psalmist offers us a way to extend this insight beyond the confines of humanity. Psalm 8 describes the majesty of God as it ponders the human place in this broad universe. What are humans compared to the magnificence of the sky, the moon, and the stars? And yet, the Psalmist declares that our lives are precious to the One who creates us and calls us into relationship with God, with one another, and with the earth. On our journey through Lent, we are invited to look to the earth and sky so that we may deepen our relationship with all of creation. As we see our identity as bound up with that of the earth, we discover our future as that which belongs to God.

_____

_____

_____

_____

_____

_____

Day 21

"In my distress, I called upon the Lord... God came swiftly on the wings of the wind." Psalm 18:6 and 10b

Last year, we hung a wind chime on our porch so that we could enjoy the sound it makes when the breeze blows through our yard. However, on many nights when the wind is blowing steadily, I go out on the porch and detach the center section of the chime so that we won't have to listen to its steady, insistent sounds. For the Psalmist, though, the sound of the wind provides a reminder of the promise of God's faithfulness. The rustle of the trees as the wind steadily blows serves as a call to prayer. In times of turmoil when the Psalmist cries out for help, he experiences God's presence as the One who comes on the wings of the wind.

Like us, the Psalmist acknowledges that at times he feels God's absence in his life. He looks at his life and the world around him and wonders: where are the signs of God's presence? As reassurance, he turns to the familiar senses in the world around him in order to see that God has not abandoned him in his time of need. As sure as the wind blows through the branches of the trees, the divine presence is woven into and through our lives and the world around us.

This Lenten season as we learn to pay closer attention to the world around us by reflecting on the elements of creation each day, we are cultivating the practice of learning to recognize God's presence in our lives. May the steady ring of the wind chime on my porch and the blowing of the breeze as you walk out your front door cause us to pause for a moment and give thanks for God's faithful presence in our lives.

_____

_____

_____

_____

_____

_____

Day 22

"Make a joyful noise to God, all the earth; sing the glory of God's name; give to God glorious praise."
Psalm 66:1-2

The sounds of nature rise up from the earth and surround us. The birds call to one another from the tree branches; the crickets chirp from their hiding places in the tall grass. The earth is a home teeming with life of all varieties. Buzzing bees fly past us and light on the flowers in our garden and the flies irritate us as they whiz around. Is it possible to consider the sounds of the earth as a praise band that offers a continuous chorus of thanksgiving to God? The Psalmist points us in this direction with these words: "All the earth worships you; they sing praises to you, sing praises to your name" (v. 4).

When we start to think about the sounds of the earth in this way, then we hear things differently. The call of the birds urges us to offer thanks for the gift of this day; the sound of the wind blowing through the trees reminds us of the Spirit's presence that moves across the face of the earth; the noisy cries of the cicadas in the trees offers a blessing on all those who walk by.

On this Lenten pilgrimage with the earth we are learning to pay close attention to our senses as sources for deepening our awareness of God's presence in us, with us, and around us. Today we celebrate the ways in which nature bursts forth in song and invites us to raise our voices in thanksgiving for the gift of life. When we offer our joyful noise as part of the cacophony of praise then we join the chorus of creation to confess our dependence on God as the creator and sustainer of life.

_____

_____

_____

_____

_____

_____

Day 23

"God turns a desert into pools of water, a parched land into springs of water." Psalm 107:35

Today marks the halfway point of our journey through Lent. It is easy to become overwhelmed by the scale of the environmental challenges that we are facing and abandon our effort to live in close relationship with the earth. When we ground our response in the context of our baptismal vows, then we begin to recognize that it not our task to save the earth but our calling to live in relationship with creation. The water of baptism that runs down our foreheads and claims us as beloved children of God awakens us to live in a community that promises to care for the earth.

The Psalmist points us towards the source of hope in the midst of our actions on behalf of the earth. The pools of water that bubble up in the desert and bring forth new life and the springs that come up to quench the thirst of the land are not the works of our hands, but the work of God. We see here a delicate balance between acknowledging God as the source of life and accepting our responsibility for harming and polluting the earth as well as assuming credit for the hard work that we do to bring healing to the earth. When we hear the words of Psalm 107 in the context of our baptismal vows to live in community with one another and in harmony with the earth, then we can give up the impossible task of desperately trying to fix everything and instead focus on the opportunities that we have each day to care for the earth.

Our daily actions are important as are our prayers for the Spirit to renew the face of the earth.

_____

_____

_____

_____

_____

_____

Day 24

"For you shall go out in joy and be led back in peace; the mountains and the hills before you shall burst into song, and all the trees of the field shall clap their hands." Isaiah 55:12

How do you feel when you watch the sun set as the colors change hue and the rays of the sun pierce through the clouds? How do you feel when you touch the morning dew on your shoes, or you catch a draft of a cool summer breeze on your face? When we stop to notice the beauty of the world around us, then we are struck by the wonder of it all from the tiny wildflowers to the snowy mountaintops. The wildness of nature causes us to catch our breath and to stand in awe before it. In spite of all of our best efforts, we simply cannot control it. It confounds us with its beauty, ferocity, diversity, and violence. We prefer to romanticize nature or to keep it in its place at the edges of our civilized world.

The prophet Isaiah offers us a different arrangement. Instead of conquering nature, how could we live in harmony with it? Can we as humans even begin to imagine receiving approval from the created world? The answer is found in cultivating joy and peace in our lives. When we go forth in joy with a sense of anticipating God's goodness and when we come home in peace having sought the well-being of our neighbors and the protection of the earth as God's good creation, then the trees around us will give us a standing ovation! Such a word of promise prompts us to look at the trees around us in a different way and to anticipate the day when they bow to offer their thanks for the peace that is breaking forth in our lives.

_____

_____

_____

_____

_____

_____

Day 25

"Listen to me, you that pursue righteousness, you that seek the Lord. Look to the rock from which you were hewn, and the quarry from which you were dug." Isaiah 51:1

Geologists study rocks in order to gain a clearer sense of the eras of evolution that have occurred on planet earth. Rocks preserve a history of life at earlier times. Fossils point to the presence of forms of life. Scientists can detect the presence or absence of water in the way that rocks are formed. Rocks offer information about the past that may also inform us about our future. The prophet Isaiah uses the lessons we can learn from rocks in a similar way. In our struggle for justice, we are not acting alone. In our search for God, we are joined by a long list of people who have gone before us and created a path for us to follow. For Isaiah, the image of a rock quarry provided a sense of shared identity. The rocks that were cut out of a larger boulder still shared the same qualities with the larger rock formation. They came from a geological era in the earth's formation in which heat and pressure combined to form this rugged material. In this portrait, rock offers us a sense of lineage and shared likeness that allows us to endure. Isaiah turns from this image to remind us of our kinship with Abraham and Sarah, the great models of faithfulness.

During this season of Lent, when we turn to the earth to reflect on God's presence around us and as we commit to care for the earth's resources and for the ways in which the earth points us to the divine presence, we take courage from all those who have gone before us to work to preserve the beauty and grandeur of creation. We draw from their stories and strengths in the hope and belief that we are hewn from the same rock.

_____

_____

_____

_____

_____

_____

4th Sunday in Lent

"Give us this day our daily bread." Matthew 6:11

There's enough for today. What is this obsession that we have of hoarding possessions and of trying to make sure that we have everything lined up for the future? When we do this, then we pretend that we hold our destiny in our own hands. We tell ourselves that we have provided for ourselves all that we will need. In the Lord's Prayer, Jesus invites us on a different path. Here, the goal is to accept the gift of each day as it comes to us and to trust that God will hear and receive our request for daily bread.

It seems like such a simple step to take. When we look around and start observing the world, then we see that much of life works in this basic way. The plants rooted in the earth that we walk by each day depend on the sun and rain for their basic nutrients. The birds that chirp from the trees in our yards go out foraging for their food each day. There is much to learn when we take time to pay attention to the rhythms of creation.

To pray these words, "Give us this day our daily bread," is an important first step of releasing ourselves from a culture that is obsessed with accumulating too much of everything. It is also a critical step in our lifelong journey of recognizing that our lives both in this moment and in the future are entrusted into the hands of God. Each meal is a blessing from God who invites us to share with our neighbors, especially those who are poor. It is enough not only to sustain us, but to relieve us from our anxieties and orient us towards a way of life that grows out of God's faithfulness.

_____

_____

_____

_____

_____

_____

Day 27

"The heavens are telling the glory of God; and the firmament proclaims God's handiwork." Psalm 19:1

Today's Scripture invites us to listen to nature. Most of the time when I go on walks, I pay attention primarily to what I see: on the one hand I notice flowers blooming and giant trees whose canopies provide shade or on the other hand I see the earth's scars where we have clear-cut trees and paved over tracts of land in the name of progress. For the Psalmist, though, creation offers us a series of sermons that invite our response.

The sky speaks to us of God's majesty and the firmament testifies to God's work in creation. The word firmament is also used in the opening section of the creation account in Genesis 1 where after creating light we read that, "God said, Let there be a firmament in the midst of the waters, and let it divide the waters from the waters" (vs. 6, KJV). In Genesis, God speaks creation into being – the light, the firmament, the waters, and the earth.

The Psalmist transposes this spoken word of God in fashioning creation to the language that the elements of nature proclaim to us. How often, though, do we stop to listen to the sounds of the world? We are so often bombarded by the sounds of our technological gadgets and our fast-paced life that we tend to shut ourselves off from the noise that surrounds us. The Psalmist invites us to tune our ears to the sounds of the earth, to allow the vastness of the sky and the immenseness of the universe to speak to us about God's presence that surrounds us. The Psalmist describes it as an endless speech (vs. 2) that continually testifies to us about the work of the Creator. May the Spirit help us to open our ears so that we may hear and respond to this witness.

_____

_____

_____

_____

_____

_____

Day 28

"Then God said to me, 'Prophesy to the breath, mortal, and say to the breath: Thus says the Lord God: Come from the four winds, O breath, and breathe upon these slain, that they may live.'"
Ezekiel 37:9

The prophet Ezekiel is looking for signs of life. In this famous passage of his vision of the valley of the dry bones, he simply wonders if there is any hope for the future. He looks out across an arid valley that is littered with dry bones and is gripped by a sense of despair. When God asks him if these bones can live, he simply responds that only God knows. The text for today offers us two key insights: 1) that our future lies solely in God's hands; and 2) that our future is integrally connected to all forms of life.

First, Ezekiel's vision invites us to place our hope for the future not in our own ability or in new scientific or technological advances, but solely in God's ongoing commitment to breathe new life into places that seem to be void of hope. In the valley of death, Ezekiel gains a glimpse of God bringing forth new life.

Second, the vision of this new life shows the way that all life is connected. The four winds bring the breath that restores life to the dry bones. As the earth breathes, so we share its breath.

Thus, the choices that we make each day of caring for the earth and protecting the quality of the air that we breathe are choices that immediately affect our own lives. Acknowledging our trust in God connects us to the source of creation and prompts us to respond to the needs of the earth. God's gift of new life draws on the resources of creation – on the healing wind that allows the planet and all that lives to breathe.

_____

_____

_____

_____

_____

_____

Day 29

*"The earth, O Lord, is full of your steadfast love;
teach me your statutes."* Psalm 119:64

The Psalmist suggests that we can learn the ways of God by paying attention to the earth. Since the earth is filled with the faithful presence of God's abiding love, we can learn about God by turning to carefully observe the world around us. For example, think about the ways in which the seasons of the year model a rhythm of growth and rest. Sabbath practices of rest are observable in the lives of flora and fauna as they go through periods of rest and renewal.

During these days in Lent we watch closely for the signs of new life on the branches of trees, and we wait patiently for the colorful eruption of spring flowers that dazzle our senses. By paying close attention to the earth, we are also learning more about God's ways which for the Psalmist provide the pathway to happiness (vs. 1). This portrait of happiness comes with a commitment to the flourishing of all the earth. Plants, animals, and humans look for harmonious ways to share this good earth. As we observe these limitations to the human temptation to dominate the earth, then we find that the ways of God are taking root in our hearts.

How can you make changes in what you take from the earth and in what you consume from the earth that will allow you to live in harmony with the earth? What are you willing to start working on today? What will you change that represents your commitment to become more closely aligned with God's ways? The Psalmist points us in the direction of happiness as we learn to accept and respect what the earth is teaching us.

_____

_____

_____

_____

_____

_____

Day 30

"The wilderness and the dry land shall be glad; the desert shall rejoice and blossom; like the crocus it shall blossom abundantly and rejoice with joy and singing. Strengthen the weak hands and make firm the feeble knees. Say to those who are of a fearful heart, 'Be strong, do not fear!'" Isaiah 35:1-2a and 4a

Today is the day to take in the beauty of the earth and to rejoice with it! How will we join in the gladness of the earth as it blossoms? As trees around us begin to bud in Spring and as the flowers begin to grow and prepare to dazzle us with their brilliant colors, the earth is beginning its annual season of rebirth. The prophet Isaiah depicts this as a choral symphony that invites our participation.

On this long journey through Lent, the goodness of the earth serves as a source of encouragement to us. It is the earth's song of renewal that revitalizes our tired hands and legs and gives us the courage to continue walking the way of the water. We gain strength for the days ahead by observing the resilience of the earth and joining in its song of joy.

The courage to change our ways that harm the earth starts by paying attention to the rhythms of nature. Learning to pause and rest as well as sensing when to grow is mirrored for us in the earth's cycles. Isaiah declares to us that we will see God's glory as we pay attention to the earth's renewal. With the earth as our guide, we can step forward with a new sense of hope. Walking in harmony with the songs of the earth helps us orient ourselves towards relationships that rejoice in the health and welfare of all creation.

_____

_____

_____

_____

_____

_____

Day 31

"They shall all sit under their own vines and under their own fig trees, and no one shall make them afraid." Micah 4:4

The vision of a new life can be glimpsed by looking at the vines and trees around us. The prophet Micah anticipates a day of promise coming in which people will return to God. They will stream to the holy mountain to take in God's word. There they will find comfort in the lush green groves that provide shelter. In the shade of the trees, their anxiety and fear will be set aside.

On this journey through Lent, we turn to nature as a place to experience the divine presence and as a resource to help us more clearly ground our lives. Trees offer us important life lessons. Perhaps we should not only hear this text as a word of hope for the future, but also listen to the way that it points us to places where we may find rest today. What is it about trees that helps us relax? In the hot summer weather, trees provide us with shade. When we place our hands on the tree trunks, the weathered texture of the bark speaks to us about endurance. Their green branches offer us lessons about renewal and their twisted branches show us that even in difficult circumstances there is growth in new directions.

Today we are invited to let go of our fears and to trust in the One who created the vines and trees and who accompanies us on our journey. The trees that we walk past each day offer us their silent witness of the Creator's love for this world. In the beauty of their branches that ripple in the wind, we find hope for today and a promise for tomorrow.

_____

_____

_____

_____

_____

_____

Day 32

"Everyone who hears these words of mine and acts on them will be like a wise man who built his house on rock." Matthew 7:24

Many of us learned to sing these words from Jesus's parable when we were young: the wise man built his house upon the rocks and the rain came tumbling down. In Matthew, these words of Jesus are part of the sermon on the mount. For Matthew, it is a collection of Jesus's teachings from the beginning of his public ministry that challenges the status quo. Blessed are the poor in spirit, those who mourn, the meek, those who long for justice, those who show mercy, and those who work for peace. It is not the kind of list of successful traits that one finds on the covers of magazines or in the pages of self-help manuals. And yet, Jesus declares that these virtues are the primary ones in God's reign because they provide a foundation that will stand the test of time. They are like a wise man who builds on rock instead of sand.

We grasp rocks because they are solid. They don't simply sift through our fingers; their firmness points to a form of permanence. Rocks offer us deep truths. They invite us to ask ourselves about our levels of commitment and the ways in which we are structuring our lives. How does Christian faith figure into our daily lives? In what ways does Jesus's invitation to a blessed life figure into our decisions? Today you are invited to pick up a rock, hold it in your hand, and allow the rock to present the question of how we are building our lives. Are we building on sinking sand or on a solid foundation?

5th Sunday in Lent

"Day by day, as they spent much time together in the temple, they broke bread at home and ate their food with glad and generous hearts, praising God and having the goodwill of all the people." Acts 2:46-47a

This description of the early Christian community provides us with key insights for our lives today. First, these followers of Jesus spent time in daily prayer. Each day they gathered at the temple to participate in the regular cycles of prayer that sustained their lives of faith. Second, they joined together in sharing meals that provided a sense of community as well as a sense of joy. Third, they worked for the well-being of all those in their community by reaching out to those in need and invited them to join them. It was these simple acts that caused the Christian movement to grow rapidly. In fact, Luke writes that day by day God added to their number.

Our journey through Lent starts with an awareness of God's presence in the world around us and leads to a growing sense of gratitude for God's grace in our lives. In the Gospel and in Acts, Luke attaches these insights to the regular practice of breaking bread together. Luke describes this often with particular words: Jesus took bread, blessed and broke it, and gave it to others to share. In Church, we call this practice "eucharist" which is the Greek word for thanksgiving. This is the defining action in what we call the Lord's Supper – the sacrament in which we share bread and cup together. In Acts 2, this meal is a daily act and a daily opportunity for thanksgiving and celebration. For these first Christians, the daily act of breaking bread and sharing it in community leads to glad and generous hearts. As we gather on this day to break bread, may we also experience Christ's presence and share what we have with all who are in need.

_____

_____

_____

_____

_____

_____

Day 34

"Your steadfast love, O Lord, extends to the heavens, your faithfulness to the clouds." Psalm 36:5

We are often tempted to make God's love and salvation focus solely on our ourselves. Notice the way we often talk about being called and chosen by God and the times in which we seem to place ourselves in a special category. The Psalmist provides an important corrective perspective to our preoccupation with our own plight. God's love extends to the heavens and God's faithfulness envelops the clouds that float across the sky. God's salvation includes humans and animals alike (vs. 6). When we begin to see ourselves as part of the grand scheme of creation (and not as the primary focus of it), then we begin to grasp that the invitation to care for the earth as part of our Christian discipleship involves accepting the role that we as humans play within a deeply relational understanding of the earth. This shift in perspective requires us to confess the times in which we have interpreted the language of "dominion" (Genesis 1:26 where God gives humanity dominion over the earth) as permission to conquer, exploit, and abuse the earth as a resource made for our own enjoyment and disposal. In contrast, the Psalmist portrays the ways in which our own existence is interconnected with the forms of life that surround us. The well-being of plants and animals, of the sky and the air are significant because God's love extends to them as well as to us. As we begin to make these connections, then the Psalmist's words point us to God as the source of all life: "For with you is the fountain of life; in your light we see light" (vs. 9). This Lenten journey offers us the chance to see ourselves along with all of creation as recipients of divine love and grace.

_____

_____

_____

_____

_____

_____

Day 35

"For lo, the one who forms the mountains, creates the wind, reveals his thoughts to mortals, makes the morning darkness, and treads on the heights of the earth – the Lord, the God of hosts, is his name." Amos 4:13

We don't often think of the howling wind as a sign of God's presence. More often than not we try to defend ourselves from its power. When it is cold outside, we bundle up in layers to protect ourselves from the wind. When the wind blows the rain sideways, we turn our backs and scurry inside to avoid the effects. We wait for it to die down, so we can enjoy a calm day.

In contrast, the prophet Amos finds in the power of the wind a sign of God's presence that is linked to the possibility of our discovering the diverse ways in which God is revealed to us. Amos sees and feels these possibilities in the beauty of the mountains, the blowing of the breeze, and the shadows in the morning before the sun rises and begins to warm the earth. For Amos, these daily occurrences of power and beauty in the world around him are woven into his experience of God's call. They come as both signs and warnings of God's presence and proclamation to "seek me and live" (5:4).

Perhaps we can learn from Amos a deeper appreciation of the world around us that looks for God's presence not only in the moments of beauty, but also in times of chaos and uncertainty. Scientists describe the role of wind as that which allows the earth to achieve a sense of equilibrium by moving air from high pressure to low pressure systems. When we tune into this flow of nature then we begin to discover ways in which the rhythms of nature point us toward seeing and responding to the Creator.

_____

_____

_____

_____

_____

_____

Day 36

"For as the earth brings forth its shoots, and as a garden causes what is sown in it to grow up, so the Lord God will cause righteousness and praise to spring up before all the nations." Isaiah 61:11

During this journey through the season of Lent, the earth offers us signs of hope in the goodness of God. The prophet Isaiah sees these possibilities by turning to look at the world around him. The growth of the tree branches offers signs of new life; the produce of the garden provides food for us to eat. These observations of the world are the source of hope that God will bring justice to the earth even in times of uncertainty. When the earth thrives, then it serves as a source by which all of life can prosper.

Isaiah links this basis for hope to the work of the Spirit that calls us to specific tasks: "to bring good news to the oppressed, to bind up the brokenhearted, to proclaim liberty to the captives, and release to the prisoners" (vs. 1). It is a vision of new life in which we come together to work for those who are marginalized in our communities. And it is worth noting that this vision of new life served as the text for Jesus's first sermon in his home synagogue in Nazareth (Luke 4:18).

Today we can see ways in which our prayers for justice and praise are visible in the trees, plants, and bushes that provide us with oxygen, shade, food, and beauty. As we welcome strangers, provide for the poor, give shelter to immigrants, and tend to the sick, we are participating in God's vision of earth where life is shared together. Let's take hope from the signs of nature springing up around us and let us serve as sources of hope to all who are in need.

_____

_____

_____

_____

_____

_____

Day 37

Then the eyes of the blind shall be opened, and the ears of the deaf unstopped; then the lame shall leap like a deer, and the tongue of the speechless sing for joy. For waters shall break forth in the wilderness, and streams in the desert; the burning sand shall become a pool, and the thirsty ground springs of water; Isaiah 35:5-7a

Freedom for one is freedom for all! Our passage from Isaiah 35 links the liberation of those who are marginalized with the renewal of the earth. The restoration of sight to the blind, of hearing to the deaf, and of healing to the lame are integrally connected to the well-being of all the earth.

We can see that the front lines of pollution and toxicity have always been borne by people of poverty. From the native people of South Dakota who fought the pipeline expansion across their own land to the inner-city poor who continue to suffer the health consequence of lead pipes and toxic water in places like Flint, Michigan, we have seen the devastating effects of reckless development and corporate greed. Caring for the earth must always be related to responding to the needs of those who are poor and on the margins of our communities. Responding to those who struggle each day to survive is connected to caring for the earth's health. In Isaiah, the earth rejoices at the deliverance of the poor. Human healing is integrally connected to the earth's abundance. One action leads to another: our care for those who are poor prompts the earth to share the joy of those who experience healing and relief. This deep notion of interdependence shows the way in which our care for our neighbors creates an effect that ripples through the world.

_____

_____

_____

_____

_____

_____

Day 38

"On either side of the river is the tree of life with its twelve kinds of fruit, producing its fruit each month; and the leaves of the tree are for the healing of the nations." Rev. 22:2

A tree stands at the center of John's closing vision in the book of Revelation. Next to the river of life grows a tree that provides sustenance and healing for all people. The tree produces fruit every month in order that there is abundant food for all to share. Not only does the tree provide ample produce, but it also provides the leaves that are the source of healing for all who come to partake of it. This vision is naturally a return to the Garden of Eden – the place of our origin and exile and the place that we destroyed long ago. It points us towards a new paradise, a place where we finally realize our dependence on the earth not as a place to dominate and consume but as a place to find a home to share with all that God created.

This season of Lent offers us the gift of re-orientation. This journey helps us to see the ways in which our spiritual and physical health are inextricably intertwined. Caring for the earth is a Christian responsibility that equally feeds our body and soul. Tending to the trees in our yards and neighborhoods points us toward the vision of a renewed earth where we learn to live in harmony with the planet.

Awakening to the beauty of the trees around us and offering thanks for their abundant gifts offers us a way to live into the biblical narratives in which trees (and all of nature) have such a central role. Let us give thanks for trees and all that they provide us.

_____

_____

_____

_____

_____

_____

Day 39

"Blessed is the king who comes in the name of the Lord! Peace in heaven, and glory in the highest heaven!' Some of the Pharisees in the crowd said to him, 'Teacher, order your disciples to stop.' Jesus answered, 'I tell you, if these were silent, the stones would shout out.'" Luke 19:38-40

The religious leaders who opposed Jesus's message ordered him to silence his followers when they greeted him as he rode into Jerusalem. Their shouts of hosanna were in recognition of Jesus as the One who brings God's presence into the world. Their cries were a call for peace to descend from the heavens above and take root in their lives. And yet even these prayers for peace were received as a threat to those who were in positions of power and privilege.

Jesus's response to the calls for silence was to announce that God's presence was known by all of creation. Even the rocks would shout out and confirm that all of creation points to God's glory. In these days of endless debate and incessant bickering, maybe we should turn the sound down on our media devices and begin to listen to the rocks that we pick up on our walks through the woods, along the riverside, or at the beach. To be able to listen to the rocks requires that we grow silent and tune our ears to the world around us. What do you think that rocks tell us? A geologist is able to pick up a rock and see the history of the world. A jeweler might be able to discern in a rock a form of beauty that dazzles our eyes. Each of us will find something different in the witness that rocks provide and yet each of us can discern a way in which even a rock points us to the truth of God's good creation.

_____

_____

_____

_____

_____

_____

Palm/Passion Sunday

"Very truly, I tell you, unless a grain of wheat falls into the earth and dies, it remains just a single grain; but if it dies, it bears much fruit." John 12:24

Creation provides us with images of ways to live our lives. By learning to pay close attention to the world around us, we can glean insights from the cycles of nature where death and life exist side by side. Grains of wheat are buried in the ground and then over time with the gifts of water and sunshine grow up to produce a crop that provides us with bread.

On Palm Sunday, we celebrate the story of Jesus's triumphant entry into the city of Jerusalem where he is greeted by the crowds waving branches and shouting out blessings of hosannas to this one who comes in God's name. In the midst of this joyous event, Jesus offers his followers a surprising word. Our lives are to be like grains of wheat planted in the earth in order that there will be growth. For Jesus this is not simply a metaphor, but a way of life that he is experiencing. John describes it vividly: Jesus sets his face towards Jerusalem; Jesus hands himself over to his accusers; Jesus lays down his life for his friends; Jesus bows his head and gives up his spirit. These dramatic actions portray the life that Jesus invites us to follow in this passage from John's Gospel. We are invited to leave self-preservation behind and to invest our lives by pouring them out in serving one another and in caring for creation. What will we do with this gift of life? How will we choose to spend our time, energy, and resources? The Gospel invites us to plant our lives with the hope that through faithful acts of love that God will provide a bountiful harvest.

_____

_____

_____

_____

_____

_____

Holy Monday

"Shower, O heavens, from above and let the skies rain down righteousness; let the earth open, that salvation may spring up, and let it cause righteousness to sprout up also; I the Lord have created it." Isaiah 45:8

On Palm Sunday, we noted that the crowd used tree branches to welcome Jesus on his triumphal entry into Jerusalem, waving them in tribute to the One who comes in the name of God.

Today's text from Isaiah extends this in a way that shows the earth as an active participant in the healing and renewal of creation.

Isaiah portrays the earth as leading the way. The skies open up and rain down righteousness as it brings renewal to the parched earth. The earth opens up so that healing waters spring up to bring growth and refreshment to all that surrounds this oasis.

Isaiah describes this verdant portrait as providing two key testimonies. First, the earth's fertility is integrally connected to righteousness. Our commitment to protect and care for the earth is a way of working for justice in creation. For Isaiah, the earth itself provides both a witness and a source of the wholeness of life that God envisions for all of creation. The earth and sky collaborate to prompt in us a longing for justice in the world around us. Second, these elements of nature point to God's presence as the Creator.

Isaiah describes the salvific presence of creation as the result of God's action. Righteousness springs up in the world and in our lives as the result of God's commitment to bring regeneration and renewal to us and to all of creation. In church, we describe this as sacramental signs of God's presence in the gifts of water, bread, and wine that participate in our call to renewal and point to God's grace that sustains us on our journey.

_____

_____

_____

_____

_____

_____

Holy Tuesday

"The wind blows where it chooses, and you hear the sound of it, but you do not know where it comes from or where it goes. So it is with everyone who is born of the Spirit." John 3:8

Wouldn't it be great to have all of the answers to life figured out? We often wish that we could simply make a short checklist and have everything wrapped up to put in a nice box. Whenever we are tempted to believe that we have it all sorted out, then life throws us a curve and we discover once again this mysterious gift called life. In today's Scripture, Jesus reminds us of our inability to control our destiny (no matter how hard we try). Jesus describes this insight in terms of the way that we experience the wind blowing. It simply does. We can hear it, but we don't know where it come from or where it goes.

To be born of the Spirit is to receive the gift of new life that comes when we recognize our dependence on God as the source of life. In turning to the mysterious presence of wind that blows across our lives, Jesus encourages Nicodemus to give up his search for a rational explanation of his life and place his future in the hands of God. As we move through these days of Holy Week that lead to Jesus's crucifixion in Jerusalem, we are tempted to try to find a way to describe these tragic events that will make sense of them. Instead, the Gospel invites us to accept the possibility that in the midst of our uncertainty God is at work. Even as we learn to brace ourselves and accept the wind as an integral part of the design of nature, so too may we come to see ourselves as dependent on the One who creates and breathes life into us.

_____

_____

_____

_____

_____

_____

Holy Wednesday

"Jesus spat on the ground and made mud with the saliva and spread the mud on the man's eyes, saying to him, 'Go wash in the pool of Siloam.'"
John 9:6-7

John's Gospel offers us the story of the healing of a man who was born blind. Jesus brings healing to the blind man by mixing together dirt and spit that he rubs on the man's eyelids as he instructs him to wash in the water at the pool of Siloam that was built by King Hezekiah to serve as a source of water for the ancient city of Jerusalem (II Kings 20:20). For John, this miracle serves as one of the seven signs that point to Jesus as the chosen one who reveals God to us.

It is interesting to note that Jesus's healing of the man involves the earth. Here the earth is a resource for human healing. The story is intended to remind us of where we came from. In the creation stories of Genesis, God creates man from the dust of the earth before breathing life into him (Gen. 2:7). Jesus's miracle of new creation relies on the same source for the healing of the man who was previously unable to see.

Both of these creation stories portray the earth itself as a source of our life and our healing.

What if we looked at the earth as the source of our lives and as the resource for our healing? How might we treat the earth when we recognize our dependence on it for our existence? Caring for the earth is not just a nice thing to do, it is ultimately an act of self-care in which our sense of sight is deeply connected to the well-being of the earth.

Holy Thursday

"Then Jesus poured water into a basin and began to wash the disciples' feet and to wipe them with the towel that was tied around him." John 13:5

Jesus took a pitcher of water and poured it into a basin so that he could wash the feet of his disciples. This simple and surprising act drew on the custom of his day where often servants washed the feet of those who came into the house.

At the end of a long day of travel and walking around the dusty streets, it was a necessary custom to clean up as part of the preparation for an evening meal. The surprising part of the story is that Jesus as the leader of this movement took it on himself to do the washing. Jesus's action embodies his life of service and care for those around him and comes with specific instructions: "For I have set you an example, that you also should do as I have done to you" (vs. 15).

It is worth noting that this act of foot washing assumes the availability of clean water. The act of cleansing one's dirty feet requires a source of fresh water. No one wants to stick their toes into a basin of polluted water. As we walk by and for the water on this journey through Lent, we are coming to see the ways in which our basic needs for clean water are closely connected to the ways in which people of faith have used water in baptisms and foot washings for centuries. For followers of Jesus, working for clean water is part of our life that begins when baptismal water is poured over us and we are declared Christ's disciples. How will you live out this baptismal promise today and in the coming weeks?

_____

_____

_____

_____

_____

_____

Good Friday

"So they took Jesus; and carrying the cross by himself, he went out to what is called The Place of the Skull, which in Hebrew is called Golgotha. There they crucified him." John 19:17-18a

Jesus was put on a tree to die. He hung there on a cross suspended between heaven and earth. The Gospels offer different depictions of this tragic event with the earth shaking and the sky turning black. It presents a stark contrast to the good news of his birth with the guiding star and the angelic announcements proclaiming peace on earth. Instead, the earth weeps and mourns with the death of this innocent man. It is an event that even the earth itself cannot escape. The cross is made from the death of a tree. Jesus's blood pours out into the soil beneath the cross. His body is taken from the cross and placed in a cave where the opening is covered by a large rock. This horrible death comes with the scarring of the earth.

On this Lenten journey we have talked about incarnation as God's presence here on earth. As Christians, we recognize the divine presence in the world around us even as we proclaim this truth particularly in the life of Jesus of Nazareth. On Good Friday, we acknowledge that crucifixion includes the desecration and destruction of the earth that God created and declared good. On this day when we lament the death of Jesus Christ, we add to our prayers and confess the ways in which we have exploited the earth's resources that has resulted in the extinction of wide numbers of species. We have contributed to the fragile state of this place we call home. Our greed, our arrogance, our unwillingness to change our ways that endanger the earth. *Kyrie eleison.* May God have mercy upon us.

_____

_____

_____

_____

_____

_____

Holy Saturday

"So Joseph took the body and wrapped it in a clean linen cloth and laid it in his own new tomb, which he had hewn in the rock. He then rolled a great stone to the door of the tomb and went away. Mary Magdalene and the other Mary were there, sitting opposite the tomb." Matthew 27:59-61

Following the death of Jesus on the cross, his body is taken by Joseph of Arimethea and prepared for burial. Joseph takes the corpse and places it in his own tomb that is carved out of a rocky hillside. Once the body is placed inside this cavelike area, then a large stone is rolled in front of the doorway. We pause on this day to reflect on how rocks provide both a place on which to lay the body of Jesus as well as a way in which to enclose, protect, and preserve his body. On Easter Sunday, we see that the stone that is rolled away disclosing the good news of Christ's resurrection. These rocks serve as central signs in the story of Jesus's death and resurrection that we are experiencing this week.

What signs do rocks serve in our lives today? How might they point us in ways that look to God's presence around us?

There are times in our lives when a particular rock takes on special meaning. We find a rock on a beach and carry it with us as a memory of that special day. At other times we look at a massive rock that provides a natural habitat for wildlife and are struck by its power and beauty. As we spend this holy Saturday in a time of waiting and lamentation for the death of Jesus and for the ongoing pain in our world, looking to the role that rocks play in the biblical story and in our own lives may provide us with a source of hope that God is not finished with this story or us yet.

_____

_____

_____

_____

_____

_____

Easter Sunday

"When Jesus was at table with them, he took bread, blessed and broke it, and gave it to them. Then their eyes were opened, and they recognized him;" Luke 24:30-31

We have travelled this long journey through the Lenten season together by learning to become aware of the gifts that the earth as God's good creation provides us. By paying attention to the elements in the world around us, we begin to see our connection with and dependence on the earth. Yet even as we grow in our awareness of God's presence in the world around us, we also sense and feel the moaning and groaning of the earth as the impact of human consumption takes an increased toll on the earth's resources. Like these early disciples in Luke's Gospel, we too face times of discouragement. We ask ourselves the question: What difference will our actions make given the massive challenges of climate change and pollution? The hopeful news of Easter is two-fold: 1) God brings forth resurrection in the midst of suffering and death. The risen Christ, who is presented to the disciples, as a mysterious stranger, accompanies us on this journey; and 2) Hope arises as we learn to connect our actions of earth care with the stories of God's presence in Scripture, creation, and our own lives. The road to Emmaus offers us a pattern for Christian living that in hearing, receiving, and devouring the Gospel our lives are transformed.

Today and in the days to come, Christ goes with us and welcomes us into living the life of resurrection, a life that is not calculated by what we think we can accomplish but erupts out of the ground of God's faithful presence that continues to bring new life to us. As followers of Jesus Christ, we are called to live out this hope in caring for all of God's creation.

A Baptismal Prayer of Thanksgiving

As followers of Jesus, we are called to work together to care for creation. Our baptismal prayers and vows serve as an important resource to sustain us on this journey. I wrote the following baptismal prayer that is part of the Book of Common Worship as a way to show the integral connection between baptism and earth care. My thanks to Westminster John Knox Press for permission to include it. (*Book of Common Worship*, 2018, p. 447)

In the beginning, when your Spirit moved over the face of the waters, light and life emerged from the dark and formless void.

At your calling, all creation came forth and you declared that it was good.

Within the presence of the same Spirit of light and life, we give thanks for the gift of water that sustains life: For the earth and the air for plants and trees, for birds and fish, for animals and humans.

In the gift of your covenant, you led your people through the Red Sea and out of slavery to freedom.

By the rivers of Babylon, you offered consolation to your people in captivity.

When Jesus was baptized in the Jordan River, all creation was blessed by you.

Through his death on the cross, Jesus' baptism became complete and in his resurrection the gift of eternal life is available to all.

We gather around this water to give thanks for the gift of birth and for the experience of new birth.

We take this water from the earth that you created, [from the local rivers of ***] to pour it over our bodies to mark us as followers of Jesus Christ, and to celebrate our calling as beloved children of God.

We give thanks for N. whose call to discipleship we celebrate in the Sacrament of Baptism.

By your Spirit, breathe new life upon those who pass through this water.

Bind them to your unending love and to the community of faith that they may share with joy this life of discipleship and mission, serving all in need.

Give them strength to follow faithfully in the way of Christ that they may serve as a sign of your redemptive love by caring for others and for the world that you created.

We praise you and thank you for your goodness that creates us, calls us, and claims us as your own beloved children.

To You, Holy One, Holy Three, be all glory and honor, now and forever. **Amen.**

CPSIA information can be obtained
at www.ICGtesting.com
Printed in the USA
JSHW022128081222
34561JS00006B/35